Quick Guide to

Analogue Synthesis

Ian Waugh

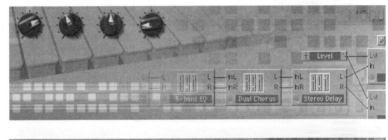

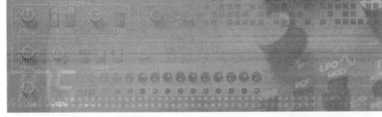

PC Pub

PC Publishing
Export House
130 Vale Road
Tonbridge
Kent TN9 1SP
UK

Tel 01732 770893
Fax 01732 770268
email info@pc-publishing.co.uk
website http://www.pc-publishing.co.uk

First published 2000

ISBN 1 870775 70 8

British Library Cataloguing in Publication Data
A catalogue record for this book is available from the British Library

Printed in Great Britain by Martins the Printers Limited

Contents

Preface

When digital synthesisers first appeared, they said analogue synthesis was dead. But it wouldn't lie down and die. So many musicians continued to clamour for analogue synths that they created a burgeoning market in second-hand models which often sold for several times their original price!

Why? Because digital synths were difficult to understand. They were almost impossible to program and the sounds weren't, well, quite as phat and phunky as analogue sounds. Oh, and you couldn't twiddle the dials and sliders to control the sounds in real-time. In other words, they simply weren't as usable. Or as much fun.

Synth manufacturers thought the analogue retro phase would die out and continued developing digital synths. But it didn't, and synth designers had to rethink their strategy. The result was digital synths which behaved as though they were analogue synths. And everyone was happy.

The recent increase in computing power has also made it possible to develop synthesisers which run entirely in software – soft synths – and these continue to be one of the major areas of music software development.

A vast number of synthesisers of both the hardware and software variety, whether they generate their sounds by digital or analogue means, use an analogue synthesis model as a front end. Even those which use an alternative type of synthesis, such as physical modelling and even FM (the first popular alternative to analogue synthesis), use many analogue-type principles.

A basic grounding in analogue synthesis is an excellent preparation for working with all forms of synthesis and this *Quick Guide to Analogue Synthesis* is designed to help get you and your synth up and running as quickly as possible. It explains what analogue synthesis is, how it works and how to program a synthesiser – of the hard or soft variety – to produce typical, classic analogue sounds as well as your own individual creations.

Dedication

To Pam and Ted,

...a perfect Synthesis...

With much love

What is analogue synthesis?

Before we start, we need to clarify just exactly what we mean by analogue synthesis.

Strictly speaking, analogue synthesis is the process of generating sound using analogue electronic circuitry. Most synthesisers today use digital circuitry but when synthesisers were first developed, analogue circuits were used because there was no alternative.

Now the term 'analogue synthesis' has broadened to include digital synthesisers which emulate their analogue counterparts – an analogue synthesiser in all but the analogue circuits, in other words. In fact, most commercial hardware 'analogue' synthesisers use digital technology and, of course, all soft synths are digital, running as they do on computers which are digital machines.

The term can also be applied more loosely to other types of synthesis which adopt controls typically used by analogue synthesisers. In such cases some controls may have readily-identifiable analogue synthesis components while other sections may be specific to the type of synthesis being used. We'll touch more upon this in a moment.

Analogue synthesis has remained popular and is at the core of many other forms of synthesis because it works well and the synthesis process follows a fairly logical path. It is, therefore, relatively easy to understand and even if you're a complete newcomer to synthesis, by the end of this book you should have a good working knowledge of the subject and be able to create your own synth patches on a range of hardware and software synths.

Analogue synthesis in a digital world

We've mentioned analogue synthesis and digital synthesisers which emulate analogue synthesisers, so what's the difference?

Analogue circuits work with voltages. As they pass from component to component, voltages are changed and modified to produce a particular result. In the case of analogue synthesis this may be the production of a waveform.

However, as you may recall from your school-day physics, electricity moves faster through materials as they increase in temperature. As circuits warm up the output may not be exactly as intended in the original design. In other words, the circuit may become a little unstable and many analogue synthesisers were notorious for drifting out of tune. The usual procedure was to leave them switched on for period of time to give the circuits time to warm up and then the synth would be tuned to other instruments.

1

An introduction to analogue synthesis

To be fair, it was mainly the very early synths which had these problems, and most models produced from the 70s onwards were relatively stable.

Digital systems work with discrete pieces of data. They output a particular result which, at the lowest level, is simply a list of numbers, 0s and 1s, and no matter how warm the chips become they still generate the exact numbers they were programmed to produce. They are, therefore, extremely stable and a digital synth will maintain its tuning whatever the temperature of its circuits.

So hooray for digital circuits, eh! Well, yes and no. Because of the small variations which crept into analogue circuitry, many analogue synths had a warmth which is not naturally present in the absolute, clinical precision of a digital circuit. This led many musicians to claim a preference for analogue technology. Today, however, synth designers have learned how to program such 'imperfections' into their designs so there's no reason why digital synths should sound any less warm than genuine analogue synths. Although some musicians may disagree...

Give a synth a bad name

Another feature of digital synths, and probably the one most responsible for giving them a bad name, was their general lack of knobs and sliders and things to twiddle. To change the sound on an analogue synth you would gently adjust a control and you'd have a pretty good idea how it would affect the sound. Even if you didn't, the control would change a particular aspect of the sound which would soon become apparent as you continued to twiddle.

Digital synths, on the other hand, had layers of menus accessed through a tiny LCD display. This was not conducive to creative synthesis and no good at all for making adjustments in real-time during a live performance. Also, many early digital synths did not try to emulate analogue synthesisers but used a different form of synthesis instead. Combine the two and you have a recipe for confusion and frustration. Digital synths may have been intrinsically more powerful but they lacked the 'hands on' appeal of analogue synths.

The infamous Yamaha DX7, quite possibly the most popular synthesiser ever made, used FM synthesis which few musicians, even today, understand well enough to create their own sounds. This was proven when it was revealed that of all the instruments returned to the factory for maintenance or repair, the vast majority still contained the original presets. Musicians simply could not fathom the complexities of the beast to create their own sounds.

Fortunately, those days are generally well behind us and most new synths coming onto the market are much easier to use and many have real-time controls you can twiddle, just like an analogue synth.

Modular synthesis

Sometimes you may hear the term 'modular synthesis', used seemingly interchangeably with analogue synthesis. As we'll see in the next chapter, sounds in analogue synthesisers are created using a series of modules or building blocks such as oscillators and filters. Some synthesisers consisted of banks of these modules in a rack and the user had to physically connect them in order to produce a sound.

Connections were made with leads or cords with a jack plug on either end and these would be used to patch part of one module to another. This led to the term 'patch' which is still used to mean a sound created in a synthesiser.

Several companies have produced modular synths including Moog, Roland and Arp although, as of writing, none of the major musical instrument manufacturers has a modular synth in its catalogue. However, modular synths are still being produced today by companies such as Doepfer and Technosaurus, although for a smaller and more specialised market. See the Appendix for details

Hardwired vs. modular

Having to create each sound from scratch with a modular system was very time-consuming and users needed a good knowledge of synthesis. It wasn't uncommon for some musicians to spend days perfecting a particular sound. The settings and connections for sounds were written down on what became known as patch sheets. At least they were written down if you were organised!

So synths were developed in which certain modules were permanently connected together – or hardwired – so that most settings would produce a sound of some sort right from switching on. There was still scope for creating different sounds but hardwiring linked essential modules in the most common way, saving time and giving the user a good step up on the ladder towards creating their own sounds.

Hardwired synths were not as flexible as modular synths but they were far faster and much easier to use. The majority of synthesisers developed from the 1970s were hardwired, particularly keyboard-based synths which needed to be easy to use for live work.

Figure 1.1: The Doepfer A-100 analogue modular synthesiser.

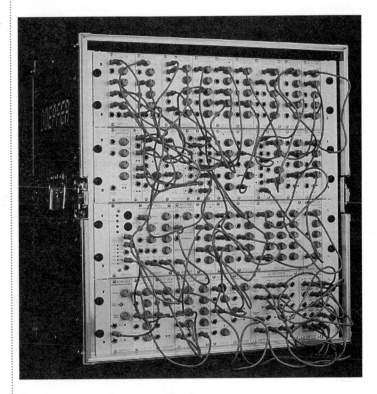

Hardware vs. software synthesisers

Essentially, a hardware synthesiser is simply a collection of dedicated circuits designed to do a particular job. It's but one short step to create a computer program that can perform the same functions (a short step perhaps, but we won't underestimate the skill and ingenuity of the programmers).

Computers have been used to generate sound for many years, although primarily in academic establishments. It wasn't until the mid-1990s that commercial software for generating sounds became available. However, because of the complexity of the process and the amount of computer processing power required, this was done off-line and the sound had to be saved as an audio file then loaded and played before you could hear it.

With the development of increasingly powerful computers in the late 1990s, developers were able to produce programs which could generate and play sounds in real-time. You could adjust a parameter and hear the resulting change instantly. And so the soft synth became a very real and viable alternative to its hardware counterpart.

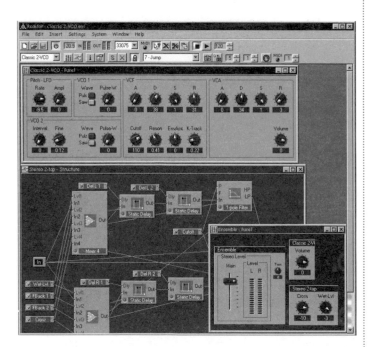

Figure 1.2: Native Instruments' Reaktor, a powerful modular soft synth which runs on both PC and Mac.

As mentioned earlier, soft synths are totally digital in nature but clever programmers have developed programs that emulate all sorts of synthesis techniques including FM, physical modelling, granular synthesis and even sampling. However, synths based upon analogue synthesis, certainly in part, remain among the most popular.

The methods and principles discussed in this book can be applied to any kind of synthesis which includes analogue-type modules. For example, a synth may generate its basic sound using, say, FM synthesis, but may then run the sound through a filter, modulate it with an LFO (low frequency oscillator) and use an envelope generator to shape it. In fact, outside academia, rare is the synth without at least a smattering of analogue parts so you should be able to use the methods described here with many types of synth.

Alternative types of synthesis

As we've already mentioned other forms of synthesis, let's end this chapter with a very brief description of some other types of synthesis you may come across. Many soft synths offer several different types of synthesis in the same package and you may even be able to mix and match different features from different synthesis methods.

The following is a list of some of the more popular types of synthesis and is not intended to be comprehensive. Don't worry if you're not familiar with some of the terms used here as they will be explained in later chapters.

Subtractive synthesis

This starts with a harmonically-rich sound and removes harmonic elements from it. This is the process most analogue synths use but any synthesis method which removes elements from a sound is using subtractive synthesis.

Additive synthesis

The addition of individual sound components to create a composite sound. Early methods combined sine waves but any kind of waveform can be used.

FM synthesis

Frequency Modulation synthesis, developed by Dr. John Chowning. It was used by Yamaha as the basis of its range of famous DX synths including the one which started the digital synthesis revolution, the DX7, in 1983. FM synthesis is quite complex and involves modulating the frequency of one waveform (the Carrier) with another waveform (the Modulator). This creates changes in the tone of the sound which doesn't make the output easy to predict. A combination of synthesis elements is known as an Operator and FM synths were typically known by the number of Operators they had. The DX7 had six while other models had four.

Physical modelling

A relative newcomer to the commercial synthesiser world, this models or emulates the processes that real-world sounds go through during their production. For example, parameters in a brass emulation might include the length and diameter of the tube and qualities of the mouthpiece. A string model might include the string diameter, its length, distance from the soundboard and even the rigidity of the pluck! The interesting thing about this is that you can combine elements from different models to create, for example, the sound of a brass instrument being plucked!

Resynthesis

As its name suggests, this involves synthesising a sound by analysing it and constructing it from the ground up, the theory being that you ought to be able to artificially resynthesise just about any sound. This was once heralded as the way forward for synthesisers but it has not found much commercial popularity yet although it is a very powerful technique.

Granular synthesis

This is another sound construction method, but one which uses extremely short segments of sound, maybe 20ms in length, known as grains. Much experimentation has been done with it in academic circles and although there are software synths which include this technique, it's another one which has escaped commercial exploitation.

Wavetable synthesis

There are actually several variant forms of wavetable synthesis but the most common one stores short samples of sounds which are repeated or looped during playback to produce longer sounds. This is very popular in PC soundcards, particularly for creating General MIDI sounds and with a good collection of samples they can be quite realistic.

Synthesis basics

This is the shortest chapter in the book because the basic analogue synthesis process is quite simple. However, it's important to know the stages that are involved because each one is responsible for a particular aspect of the sound the synthesiser generates. And even though the basic process is straightforward, it's possible to create very complex sounds.

Sound made simple

We'll skip the techy descriptions of sound and stick to the one most people know – sound is a series of vibrations. Synthesis is about the creation of sound and however that sound is produced, it will have three elements – pitch, tone and loudness. These should be self-explanatory but just to make sure there's no confusion, here's a brief description.

Pitch This is the common musical term for what is technically known as frequency and which is measured in Hertz (Hz) or cycles per second. We say Middle C – the technicians say 261.63Hz.

Tone Also referred to as timbre or tone colour, this is the quality which enables us to distinguish one sound from another when played at the same pitch and volume. It's what makes a flute sound different from a trumpet or violin. More technically, it's the harmonic content of the sound.

Loudness This is the intensity of a sound which we may refer to as volume or amplitude (technically, they're not quite the same but they're near enough for jazz). Our major concern in synthesis is how the amplitude of a sound develops over a short time period. Does it start and stop quickly like a percussive sound or does it take a while to die away like a piano note?

If we look at sound vibrations, say on an oscilloscope or by analysing the sound with a computer and displaying the waveform on screen, we can easily see two of the three attributes – frequency and amplitude. The harmonic content is not easily deduced from simple waveform displays but we'll get into all this in the next chapter.

Three steps to analogue heaven

Although the controls on some synthesisers look like the flight deck of the Concorde and the options available in some soft synths can seem overwhelming, all the sounds produced using analogue synthesis can be broken down into three basic stages:

tone generation > tone shaping > volume shaping

There is a fourth element – modulation – but this need not be present. It is used to change various aspects of a sound to make it more interesting such as creating vibrato or filter sweeps.

In analogue synthesis, the basic sound is generated with an oscillator, the tone is shaped with a filter and the volume is controlled by an envelope generator. The process follows these steps:

oscillator > filter > envelope generator

INFO

There's more about modulation in Chapter 6.

Tone generation

The oscillator generates the core sound or waveform. This is the raw material you filter, pummel and process on its journey through the other synthesiser modules. Most analogue synthesisers can generate a range of half a dozen or more basic waveforms.

The oscillator also determines the pitch of the sound although this can be modified by other synth modules and, of course, by a keyboard or a MIDI file in order to play tunes.

Tone shaping

The filter, as its name suggests, filters out parts of the waveform which results in changes to the tone. There are several types of filter which target different frequencies within the waveform and it's possible to create totally different sounds from the same raw material by judicious filtering.

Filters can also be applied dynamically to change the harmonic content of the sound in real-time, either to more accurately duplicate an acoustic sound or to create filter sweep effects.

Volume shaping

The final step is to shape the volume of the sound during its production and we do this with an envelope generator. It determines how quickly a sound reaches maximum volume and how quickly it fades away. This plays an essential part in determining how our ears interpret the sound. In fact, even if the tone colour of a sound is not quite correct, an authentic amplitude envelope can convince us of its accuracy.

Modulation

The above three attributes are responsible for the core sound but natural sounds are generally not static. The tone of a musical instrument, for example, may vary during its production and the performer may apply vibrato or pitch bend to it.

We can duplicate such effects by modulating one or more of the synthesiser modules. For example, by slowly varying the pitch we can induce vibrato. Applying a similar variation to the filter will produce an up/down filter sweep.

In the next few chapters we look at the modules used in analogue synthesis and examine the part they play in the synthesis process.

A n oscillator is at the start of every synthesiser patch. It generates a waveform, sets the pitch, and provides the raw material for the production of the sound.

The number and variety of waveforms an oscillator in an analogue synth can produce varies from instrument to instrument but there is usually a core set of three which you'll find in every synth – sine, sawtooth and square. Other common waveforms include triangle and pulse. There is often a noise generator, too, although on some instruments this may be a module in its own right.

In this chapter we look at the waveforms in detail and the type of sounds they produce.

Of cycles, peaks and amplitude

Naturally, there are a few terms associated with waveforms. A cycle is a single occurrence of a waveform and it's usually measured in Hertz (abbreviated to Hz) which is the number of times the object vibrates per second. It is also referred to as CPS – cycles per second.

Most of the waveforms used in analogue synthesis have a regular waveshape which makes their cycles easy to spot. Figure 3.1 shows a single cycle of a sine wave. The highest and lowest points are the peaks and the overall height of the waveform is its amplitude.

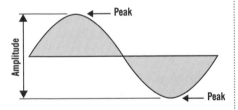

Figure 3.1: One cycle of a sine wave.

The larger the wave, from top to bottom (technically, from peak to peak), the greater its amplitude and the louder it will be. The more waves there are in a given period of time (that is, the more cycles there are per second) the higher the pitch will be.

Figure 3.2 shows three sine waves which illustrate the relationship between the waveforms and amplitude and pitch. You'll notice that the middle wave contains exactly the same number of cycles as the top one but the waves are smaller. This wave will, therefore, will be quieter than the top one.

The bottom wave has the same amplitude as the top one so it will be the same volume but there are more cycles in the same time period so it will have a higher pitch.

Figure 3.2: An illustration of pitch and amplitude. The top two sine waves contain the same number of cycles and are therefore the same pitch. However the middle one has a lower amplitude and is therefore quieter. The bottom wave contains more cycles and sounds at a higher pitch than the other two and at a similar volume level as the top waveform.

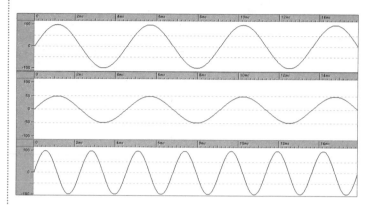

To sum up:

- The greater the height or amplitude of the wave, the louder it is.
- The more cycles there are in a given period, the higher the frequency and the higher the pitch.

Harmonics

In the previous chapter we said that sound is a series of vibrations. The simplest sound is a sine wave and that vibrates at only one frequency. It produces a clear, pure tone. Most natural objects, however, vibrate at several different frequencies at the same time. Text books use the example of an open pipe to explain how this works and it's a good example so we'll stick with it here.

As the air inside the pipe vibrates, it generates overtones called harmonics which are musically harmonious to each other. They are also commonly referred to as partials because they only form 'part' of a sound. Our perception of the pitch of a sound is derived from the lowest frequency which is known as the fundamental or first harmonic. This is also usually the strongest or loudest frequency

The additional vibrations are all at a higher rate or frequency and have a lower volume or amplitude. It's these which give a sound its tonal colour and by modifying them we can change the tone of a sound. We see how this is done in Chapter 4.

These harmonics have a simple mathematical relationship to the fundamental frequency and together they form the natural harmonic series. The third harmonic, for example, is three times the fundamental frequency, the sixth is six times the fundamental and so on. If the fundamental has a frequency of 400Hz, its third harmonic would be 1200Hz or 1.2kHz and its sixth harmonic would be 2400Hz or 2.4kHz.

We can clearly see the characteristics of pitch and loudness in a waveform but it's not at all easy to look at a waveform and know what it will sound like. Each waveshape has its own tone and theoretically there is an unlimited number of waveshapes. The best we can do is to say that the more complex a waveshape, the richer its tone colour is likely to be.

Sine waves

We've already used the sine wave in some of our examples. It contains only one waveform – its fundamental – and this is shown in Figure 3.3. It is often used for flute and drawbar organ sounds. It is also commonly used as a tuning pitch to tune other instruments and as a test tone for checking and calibrating sound analysis equipment.

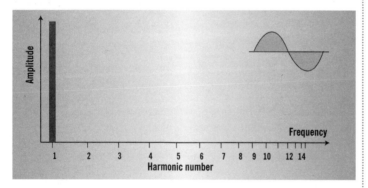

Figure 3.3: The harmonic content of a sine wave consists only of the fundamental.

Very few sounds are as simple as a sine wave. In fact, outside of a synthesiser, most sounds you're likely to hear are considerably more complex. A waveform may contain any number of harmonics, and individual harmonics may be of any amplitude. In fact, using the process of additive synthesis mentioned in Chapter 1 it's possible to create any waveshape simply by combining sine waves of different frequencies and amplitudes.

Sawtooth waves

In fact, the common waveforms you will come across in analogue synthesis could be created by adding sine waves together in specific combinations. The sawtooth wave in Figure 3.4 contains every harmonic in inverse proportion to the harmonic's number. The second harmonic has half the amplitude of the fundamental. The amplitude of the third harmonic is a third that of the fundamental, that of the fourth is a quarter of the fundamental and so on.

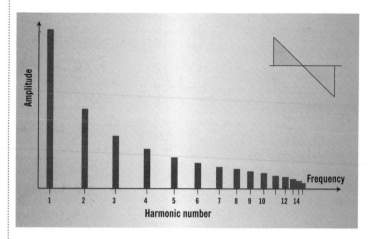

Figure 3.4: The harmonic components of a sawtooth waveform give it a rich, brassy tone.

Sawtooth waves are rich in harmonics and are used as a source for brass, strings, guitar and some woodwind sounds.

Square waves

A square wave contains only odd-numbered harmonics but with the same amplitude as those in a sawtooth wave (Figure 3.5).

Square waves produce a hollow sound and are used for woodwind sounds like the clarinet. Figure 3.6 shows the harmonic content of a typical clarinet waveform and you can see the predominance of the odd harmonics.

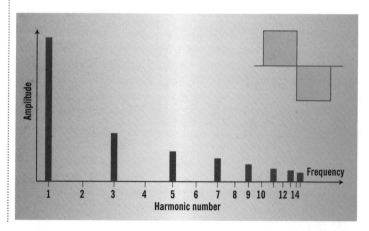

Figure 3.5: A square wave contains only odd-numbered harmonics.

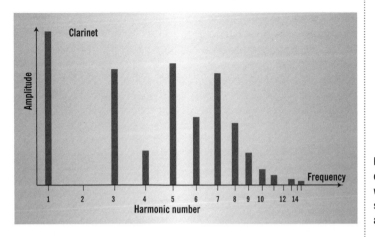

Figure 3.6: The harmonics of a typical clarinet waveform share similarities with those of a square wave.

Triangle waves

Figure 3.7 shows the harmonics of a triangle waveform which, again, is made up from odd-numbered harmonics but at much smaller levels. The relationship here is the square of the harmonic number. So the third harmonic is a ninth (3 x 3) of the amplitude of the fundamental, the fifth harmonic is 1/25th (5 x 5), the eleventh is 1/121st (11 x 11) and so on.

Although triangle waves do have harmonics, because they are not very dominant the waves sound quite mellow and near-sine like. Some synthesisers have a triangle wave instead of a sine wave.

INFO
....
Triangle waves can be used for flutes, whistles and organ sounds.

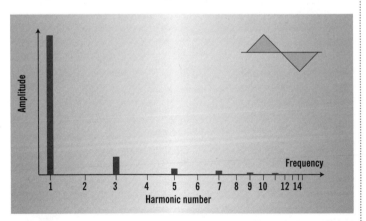

Figure 3.7: A triangle waveform contains odd harmonics at very much lower amplitudes than a square wave.

Pulse waves

The other common waveform you'll find in many analogue synthesisers is the pulse wave. At first glance it looks like an off-centre square wave – and that's just what it is. In Figure 3.5 you can see that the upper and lower portions of the square wave are the same size which is what makes it square. However, in a pulse wave, these can be varied.

The upper part of the wave is called the 'mark' while the lower part is called the 'space'. Most synthesisers have a control for adjusting the ratio between these sections which is referred to as the pulse width or the mark/space ratio. It's actually not a direct ratio between the mark and the space but rather the ratio between the mark and the complete cycle (don't blame the messenger – blame the boffins who devised the system). However, this ratio makes it easy to calculate the harmonic content.

In a square wave where the mark and space are equal, the mark is actually a half of the entire cycle so the mark/space ratio is 1:2. Think of the ratio as a fraction – 1:2 becomes 1/2 and the mark is 1/2 of the cycle. A mark/space ratio of 1:4 means the mark is 1/4 of the cycle and a ratio of 3:4 means it is 3/4 of the cycle. You can see what these waves look like in Figure 3.8.

A feature of the pulse wave is that harmonics which are multiples of the right-hand number in the mark/space ratio are absent. In the case of a square wave with a mark/space ratio of 1:2, all the even number harmonics are missing. A mark/space ratio of 1:3 would mean harmonics which are multiples of 3 – 3, 6, 9 and so on – would be missing, Figure 3.9. The amplitude of the other harmonics depends on how close they are to the missing harmonics.

As a pulse wave becomes narrower it takes on a thinner, nasal sound which can be used for oboe and harpsichord instruments although it can also be used for many other sounds such as strings and brass.

Figure 3.8: Pulse waves with different mark/space ratios.

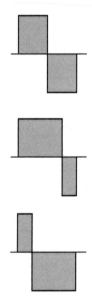

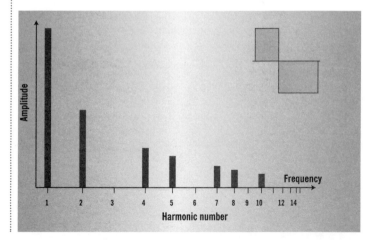

Figure 3.9: A pulse wave with a 1:3 mark/space ratio has no harmonics which are a multiple of 3.

(Really) odd harmonics

There's no law which says that a harmonic has to be a part of the natural harmonic series and be a perfect ratio to the fundamental. When they aren't, the sound can take on a slightly less harmonious edge and many metallic sounds, for example, have 'in between' harmonics. Figure 3.10 illustrates the harmonic content of a synthesised vibraphone and you can see that the harmonics are not quite 'on the line'.

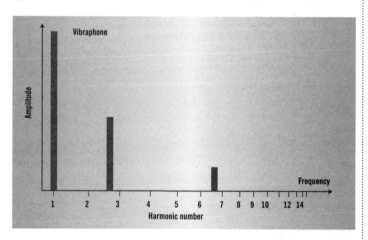

Figure 3.10: The harmonics in a vibraphone sound do not have a perfect mathematical relationship to the fundamental.

Metallic waveforms are not usually available as standard on analogue synths although some soft synths may have alternative sound sources such as an FM module or a physical modelling module. However, metallic tones can be created with standard analogue modules by modulating one oscillator with another or by combining waveforms (additive synthesis). Many analogue synths also have a ring modulation module which generates this kind of harmonic.

Metallic waveforms are used, naturally, for metallic sounds, instruments such as chimes, bells, glockenspiel, cymbals, and so on.

INFO

There's more about ring modulation in Chapter 8

Noise

The final waveforms we're going to look at are noise waveforms. The most common is white noise, Figure 3.11, which contains all audio frequencies in equal proportions. It's a hissing, rushing noise like the sound you get in between tuning radio stations.

There are, however, other 'shades' of noise of which the most popular alternative is pink, Figure 3.12. It also contains a wide range of frequencies but there are fewer higher ones and it sounds

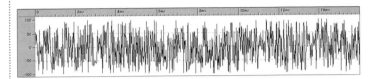

Figure 3.11: White noise contains a random combination of all audio frequencies in equal amounts and is useful for percussion and ambient sounds.

more mellow than white noise. You can create a good approximation of pink noise by knocking out a few of the higher frequencies with a low pass filter (filters coming up in Chapter 4).

Noise is often used in percussion sounds and for ambient effects such as sea and wind sounds. It can also be used as part of an instrument sound to add a breath chiff to wind instruments such as flutes.

Figure 3.12: Pink noise doesn't have as many high frequencies as white noise.

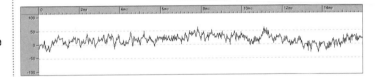

Range and tuning

As well as producing the waveform, an oscillator also determines its basic pitch. Traditionally, the pitch of an oscillator is set in 'feet' which is a throwback to the days of pipe organs when the length of an organ pipe determined its pitch – actually, they still do: these laws of physics don't change much. Typical footages will run 2', 4', 8', 16' and 32'. Each foot represents an octave and 8' is the middle octave upwards from Middle C.

Most oscillators also have tuning controls in case you need to adjust the pitch to match other instruments or simply to detune one oscillator against another. You may find a single tuning control or both fine and coarse controls.

Figure 3.13: An Oscillator from Applied Acoustics' Tassman soft synth with a range switch and both coarse and fine tune controls.

Filters

The waveforms we looked at in the last chapter provide the basic tone colour for a sound but, obviously, there are more than a handful of tone colours out there in the real world. We can change the tone of a waveform by applying a filter to it and that's what we look at in this chapter.

A filter is simply a sophisticated tone control. Almost every hi fi or CD player has bass and treble controls for adjusting the output and that's essentially what filters do, although with a little more panache.

Filter types

Filters, as their name suggests, filter out or remove certain frequencies from a waveform. There are four common filter types – low pass, high pass, band pass and band reject. Again, their names suggest what they do. A low pass filter passes low frequencies and filters out the higher ones. A high pass filter does the reverse and passes high frequencies while filtering the lower ones.

A band pass filter passes a central band of frequencies while filtering out those on either side (that is, ones which are lower than and higher than the band). A band reject filter does the opposite and filters out a central band of frequencies while passing higher and lower ones. Figure 4.1 shows how the filters affect the frequencies.

Cutoff point

The point at which a filter kicks in and starts filtering is known as the cutoff point (Figure 4.2) or cutoff frequency and this is one of the variable controls you'll find on virtually every filter.

Roll-off curves and slopes

All filters are not created equal and some are more severe than others. The more severe a filter, the greater the attenuation as the filter moves further from the cutoff point. The rate of attenuation is known as the roll-off curve or slope. A filter with a gentle slope will not attenuate frequencies further from the cutoff point as much as a filter with a steeper slope. Figure 4.2 shows some typical roll-off curves.

The roll-off curve is measured in dB/oct (decibels per octave). The decibel is a unit of measurement commonly used in recording although it doesn't often make an appearance in synthesis. A change of +6dB is a doubling of the volume and, conversely, a change of –6dB represents a halving of the volume.

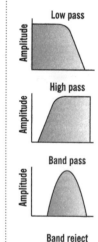

Figure 4.1: The four most common type of filter – low pass, high pass, band pass and band reject.

Figure 4.2: The more poles in a filter, the steeper the roll-off curve and the greater the frequency attenuation.

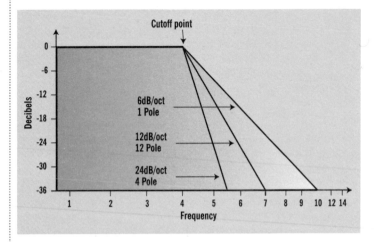

With a 6dB/oct filter, for every octave further away from the cutoff point, the signal is attenuated by 6dB – or halved, in other words. An increase in pitch of one octave represents a doubling of the frequency. The A above Middle C has a frequency of 440Hz. The A one octave higher has a frequency of 880Hz. So another way of looking at is to say that for each doubling of the frequency, the attenuation is halved.

In Figure 4.2, You can see that the 6dB/oct filter slope is the mildest because it takes longer than the others to attenuate the frequencies. The 12dB/oct filter is twice as powerful and attenuates the signal by twice as much as the 6dB filter over each octave.

The 24dB/oct slope is the most severe and you can see that you don't have to go very far beyond the first octave before the frequencies get cut short. The famous Mini Moog was one of the first synthesisers with a 24dB/oct filter which played a part in generating the 'fat' sound associated with the instrument.

Poles

INFO

As filters in soft synths are programmable, it's theoretically possible to create a filter with any slope you wish although the benefits of doing so are debatable.

The filters in hardware synthesisers contain a component called a 'pole' which determine how steep the roll-off curve will be. The more poles a filter has, the steeper the curve. Again, this is shown in Figure 4.2. Analogue synths tend to have one, two or four poles.

You might think that an ideal filter would have a response like that in Figure 4.3. However, this would immediately chop off all frequencies above the cutoff point which would sound very unnatural. Some soft synths still use the term, 'pole' while others use dB/oct.

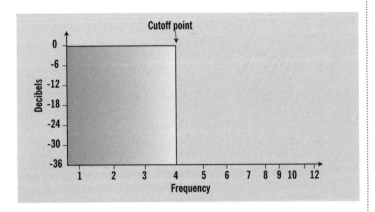

Figure 4.3: This may look
like the perfect filter on
paper but it would
produce a very unnatural
sound.

Resonance

The other major controllable parameter in a filter is resonance which is sometimes called emphasis or Q.

Resonance boosts the amplitude of the frequencies around the cutoff point. Increasing the resonance narrows the band of frequencies, targeting those around the cutoff point more tightly. Figure 4.4 shows how increasing the resonance changes the shape of the filter. Resonance is great for producing sharp filter effects and 'wow' and 'wha' sounds.

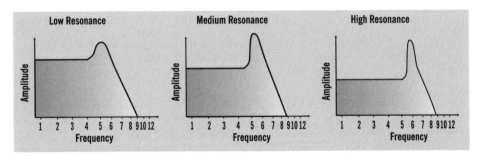

Filter feedback

On some synthesisers, including soft ones, if you crank up the resonance the filter starts to feed back on itself and generates a tone. If you control the cutoff point from a keyboard (more about this in Chapter 7) you can play this.

On older analogue synthesisers with perhaps only a couple of oscillators, this was used as an alternative sound source. On modern multi-oscillator instruments and soft synths, there is usually no need to find additional sound sources but feedback can still be useful for special effects.

Figure 4.4: Increasing the resonance boosts the frequencies around the

21

Low pass filter

The most common type of filter by far is the low pass filter. It's so common that if the term 'filter' is used without specifying a type of filter, it's a good bet that a low pass filter is being referred to.

This type of filter also produces the most natural filtering effects because in the real world, higher frequencies tend to become dampened more quickly than lower frequencies. It is the most natural filter to use with acoustic instruments.

A low pass filter attenuates frequencies above the cutoff point, Figure 4.5. It is usual to start with the cutoff point at its highest setting so all the frequencies in the waveform are passed through. Then, by lowering the cutoff point, the frequencies will be attenuated and the sound will lose its brightness. As the cutoff control is lowered, it will eventually block out all the frequencies so no sound is heard at all. However, as long as some sound is passing through the filter, the fundamental frequency will always be heard.

High pass filter

A high pass filter, Figure 4.6, works in exactly the opposite way to a low pass filter by passing the high frequencies and attenuating the lower ones. The first frequency to go will be the fundamental although you will generally still be able to tell the pitch of sound.

Because high pass filters remove the fundamental and the lower frequencies, they make a sound very thin.

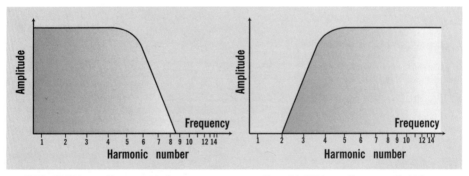

Figure 4.5: A low pass filter passes the low frequencies and attenuates the higher ones.

Figure 4.6: A high pass filter passes the high frequencies and attenuates the lower ones.

Band pass filter

A band pass filter, Figure 4.7, passes a band of frequencies both above and below the cutoff point and attenuates the others. The resulting sound will generally be thin although the filter can be used to emphasise a specific band of frequencies.

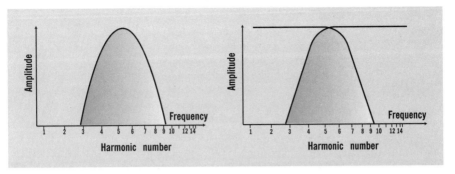

Figure 4.7: A band pass filter passes frequencies above and below the cutoff point and attenuates the rest.

Figure 4.8 Running a signal through a low pass and then a high pass filter has the same effect as applying a band pass filter.

A band pass filter can be created by passing a signal through a low pass filter and then a high pass filter, Figure 4.8. This should not be necessary with a soft synth, but not all hardware synths have a band pass filter.

Band reject filter

The final filter is a band reject filter (Figure 4.9), sometimes called a notch filter, which is an inversion of the band pass filter. It attenuates frequencies either side of the cutoff point and passes the others. As the low and high ends are both there, the result is generally a full sound but with a 'hole' in the middle. How noticeable this will be depends on the harmonic content of the source material.

If you don't have a band reject filter on your synth you can make one with a low pass and high pass filter. You run the signal through them in parallel. Figure 4.10 shows how it works.

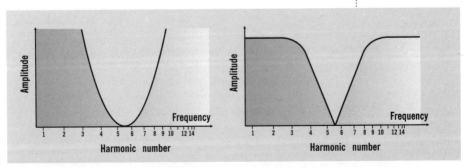

Figure 4.9: The band reject or notch filter, attenuates frequencies around the cutoff point and passes the rest.

Figure 4.10: Running a signal through a low pass and high pass filter in parallel produces a band reject filter.

5

Envelopes and amplifiers

The final stage in creating a basic sound is volume shaping. This is done with an envelope generator, sometimes called a contour generator, a transient generator or simply an ADSR, after the controls it uses.

The job of the envelope generator is to control the volume of a sound during its production (it can actually do more than this as we'll see a little later). The standard envelope generator has four phases known as ADSR – Attack, Decay, Sustain and Release - which are shown in Figure 5.1.

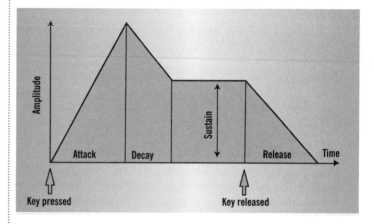

Figure 5.1: The four phases of an ADSR envelope.

It's important to understand exactly what the phases do. The main thing to realise is that three phases – Attack, Decay and Release – are a measurement of time and the fourth – Sustain – is a volume level. So we talk about Attack, Decay, and Release times but a Sustain level. Here's how they fit together.

Attack

The Attack phase is the time it takes the sound to reach a certain volume which is usually the sound's maximum volume. In a synthesiser, the Attack phase usually begins when a key is pressed or when a note is triggered.

A short Attack time will generate a percussive sound and is used for sounds such as drums, piano, vibes, and guitars. A longer attack time might be used for strings, brass instruments or a soft flute. A very long attack time is not natural to acoustic instruments but it can be used for special effects and to create backwards sounds.

Decay

The Decay phase starts immediately after the Attack phase and it's the time it takes the volume to move to the Sustain level. The

Sustain level is usually lower than the Attack level and during the Decay phase the sound usually drops in volume. The Decay phase is often longer than the Attack phase.

Sustain

The Sustain phase is a volume level and it's the level the sound "settles down" at after the Decay phase. It ends when the key is released or when the note comes to and end. Theoretically, it can last an infinite period of time although in our modern, busy world, few people are prepared to wait that long.

Release

The Release phase is the time it takes the sound to die away when the key is released. Instruments such as the vibraphone have a long release time, as do bells and gongs. Brass, woodwind and string instruments have a short release time but their sound does not cut off abruptly as does a wood block, for example.

Who needs four phases?

Using just these four phases we can generate volume envelopes similar to those produced by a vast number of natural sounds - everything from instruments to thunder and bird noises.

You'll notice that in the ADSR diagrams such as Figure 5.1 the phases are linked to a key press and key release in order to show the volume changes a note goes through during its production. There are, however, many sounds which do not use all four phases.

A wood block, for example, has an Attack phase and a Decay phase but no Sustain or Release phases, Figure 5.2. This illustrates an important difference between the Decay and Release phases. The Decay phase occurs immediately after the Attack phase. The Release phase begins when the key is released or the note ends.

The volume envelope of a wood block is independent of the length of time the key is held down. It's commonly called a one-shot sound and most drum sounds, particularly sampled drums, work the same way. When setting up this envelope, the Decay and Release times would be set to the same (short) value.

An electronic organ has Attack, Sustain and Release phases but no Decay phase Figure 5.3. The sound goes straight to the Sustain level and stays there until the key is released.

Let's look at a piano sound. If you press a key and hold it down, there is an Attack phase then during the Decay phase the sound dies away for as long as you hold your finger on the key. It has no

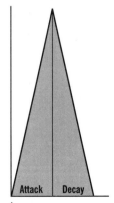

Key pressed

Figure 5.2: A wood block envelope – straight up and down.

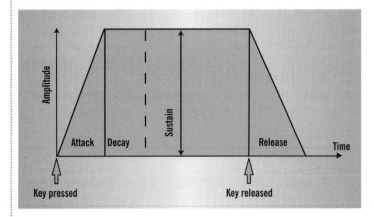

Figure 5.3: An envelope with no Decay phase could be used for an electric organ.

Sustain phase as such. If you release the key the sound dies away quickly. To set up a piano envelope you'd use a fast Attack, a slow Decay and a fast Release with no Sustain level, Figure 5.4.

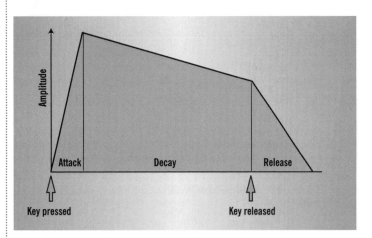

Figure 5.4: A Piano envelope has a slow Decay and fast Release.

Moving backwards

Now let's see how to create a backwards volume envelope. A sound which is played backwards sounds strange because it has a long-ish Attack phase and at the end it simply stops dead, an effect which does not readily occur in nature.

A backwards percussive sound such as a piano or a cymbal – a popular favourite in Dance music – cuts off in a most unnatural way. An envelope to create this would have a slow Attack phase and a Decay time of zero. Depending on the sound, it might have a Sustain level, too, in which case the Release time would also be

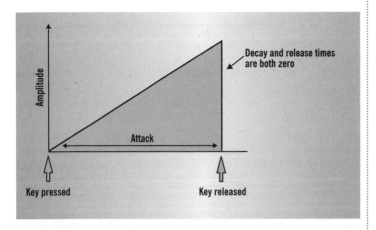

zero. Figure 5.5 shows a typically backwards envelope which could be used for a range of sounds.

The wood block and backwards envelopes have identical Decay and Release times and this raises an interesting question - what if the Release time is longer than the Decay time? Using the wood block as an example, let's see what would happen if we gave it a long Release time.

If you press and hold the key, the envelope will run through the Attack and Decay phases and the result will be the normal wood block envelope. However, if you lift the key before the Decay phase has finished the envelope will go straight to the Release phase and the sound will be prolonged. Interesting? Odd? When creating envelopes make sure that the Delay and Release times are set correctly to produce the result you want.

The amplifier

The amplifier module has been taken for granted so far. Without the amplifier there will be no sound at all. The sound generated by the oscillator runs through the filter and into the amplifier. The output from the envelope generator is fed into the amplifier which "opens" or generates a volume level corresponding to the various ADSR settings. So, the sound's volume is "shaped" during the production of the note.

An amplifier will have at least one output which is connected directly to a speaker system. It may well have an initial gain control which sets the overall volume of the output.

Pushing the envelope

So far, we've been talking about using the envelope generator to control the volume of the sound but one of the exciting aspects of modular synthesis is that a module can be used to control many other modules.

Let's see what happens if we patch an envelope to a low pass filter and make it control the cutoff frequency. We'll assume we're using a similar envelope shape to that shown in Figure 5.1. Remember that if the cutoff is closed in a low pass filter all the harmonics will be filtered out and there will be no sound.

As the envelope level rises during the Attack phase, the cutoff opens and the sound becomes brighter. The cutoff closes a little during the Decay phase so the sound becomes a little less bright. It stays like that during the Sustain phase and then the filter closes down during the Release phase. You can see how this works in Figure 5.6.

Figure 5.6: Applying an envelope to a filter can dramatically change the tone.

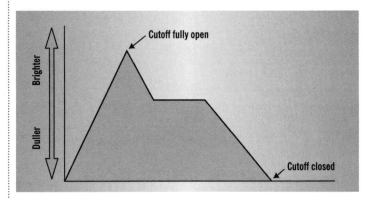

Generally, we don't want an envelope to be totally responsible for the output frequencies in this way, and most filters have an Amount control which determines how much of an external signal gets through. So instead of running the gamut of frequencies from A to Z, you can set up a more subtle, more musical effect. The tone of many instruments changes with their volume so this is a useful function to use.

Another possibility would be to patch the envelope to the oscillator to control the pitch. In Figure 5.1, if you substitute pitch for amplitude you'll have a pretty good idea what the result will be. Again, you should be able to limit the effect of the envelope so it produces a more subtle pitch blip rather than a whistle.

Other envelopes

Although the ADSR envelope is far and away the most common, there are other envelopes with different numbers and types of phases. An AD envelope provides an Attack and an automatic Decay which, as we learned earlier, is not concerned with the length of time a key is held down.

An AR envelope, on the other hand works like the organ envelope in Figure 5.3. Although there is no Sustain level as such, it is taken to be the level at the top of the Attack phase.

You may also come across envelopes with a Break point which 'breaks' a phase into two sections such as ADBDSR, Figure 5.7, which provides the opportunity for more complex contours.

INFO

There are also ADR envelopes (you can probably work out how these behave) and ADS envelopes where the Release phase (which is technically missing) is set to the same value as the Decay phase.

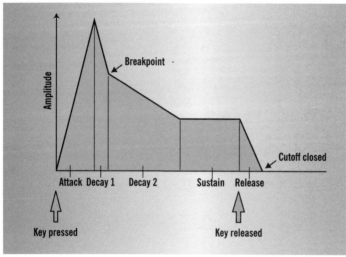

Figure 5.7: The addition of a Break point allows more complex envelopes to be constructed.

With the advent of digital technology, it became easy to construct multi-segment envelopes consisting of several phases each with their own rate and level. The DX7 was one of the first to make use of this and had four rates and levels while other instruments have even more.

If you're familiar with ADSR envelopes, multi-segment envelopes seem more complicated. If you're not, they're much easier. You simply set a target level for each phase and the time you want the envelope to take getting there. Figure 5.7 shows how this would work with a six-stage envelope. One of the interesting things you can easily do is to create envelopes where the volume rises, falls and rises again during the production of the sound.

INFO

We mention alternatives to the ADSR because you might come across them, particularly in soft synths. However, for the majority of sounds, an ADSR envelope will do just fine.

Figure 5.7: With a multi-segment envelope you can set your own rates and level.

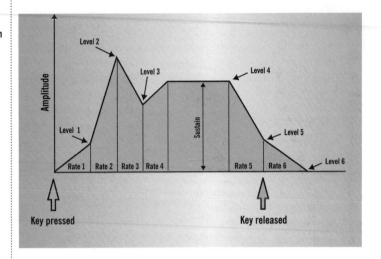

LFOs and other modulators

Using information from previous chapters, we already know enough to construct a synthesiser patch. But before we do there are a few modules which, whilst not essential, are worth looking at because they are found on most synthesisers and give character to a sound. We'll look at some additional modules in Chapter 8.

The LFO

LFO stands for Low Frequency Oscillator and apart from the oscillator, filter and envelope generator modules discussed previously, it is the most common module you'll find on a synthesiser. The LFO is similar to the audio oscillator, the main difference being, as its name suggests, the frequency at which it operates.

Audio oscillators are designed to generate waveforms which we can hear, and one with a good range might generate frequencies as low as 20Hz which is bordering on the lower threshold of human hearing. An LFO is not designed to be heard but to be used as a control signal and its upper frequency range is unlikely to be much above 30Hz and could go as low as 0.01Hz, although some LFOs may be able to generate frequencies which take several minutes to complete a waveform cycle.

LFO controls

An LFO can have several controls of which the main ones are waveform, frequency (and frequency range) also sometimes called speed, and amplitude.

The choice of waveforms is likely to be similar to those on an audio oscillator although the essential ones are sine, square and sawtooth. There may also be a triangle wave and the sawtooth may be available in both up and a down forms. This is important because the frequency of an up sawtooth rises and then falls quickly while that of a down sawtooth falls before it rises.

Some LFOs have a frequency range control as well as a frequency control. Like the range control in an audio oscillator, the range control here sets the overall frequency span while the frequency control itself offers finer control.

The amplitude, depth or amount control determines how strong the output signal is. We'll see how this can be used in a moment.

Some LFOs might also have a delay control which simply delays the signal's output. This is usually linked to a key press so the LFO kicks in a short while after a key has been pressed or a note played.

The LFO in use

So what can you do with an LFO?

Let's see what happens if we apply it to an audio oscillator. If the LFO plugs into the oscillator's frequency control, the output pitch will change according the LFO settings. If we use a sine wave with a frequency of around 7Hz the result will be a gentle variation in frequency which you will immediately recognise as vibrato.

When performers play an instrument such as a violin, particularly during slow-moving passages, they often delay the onset of vibrato and this, too, can be done if the LFO section has a delay control. It makes the vibrato sound more realistic,

If we increase the frequency the vibrato will get faster until it is no longer musical. In fact, the pitch range for musical vibrato is rather small and you can't veer too far away from 7Hz without it becoming decidedly unmusical.

If you turn up the amplitude or depth control, the size of the LFO waves will increase causing larger pitch changes until the output is like a siren.

Now, let's say we substitute a sawtooth for the sine wave. Instead of the pitch undulating to the beat of a sine wave it will rise and fall as it follows the sawtooth waveform.

Now let's try a square wave. A square wave jumps from one level to another so the audio output does likewise oscillating between two pitches. If the amplitude control on the LFO is small, the result will be a trill. Higher settings will increase the distance between the two pitches.

Using an LFO with other modules

The LFO is not restricted to modulating the audio oscillator. As is the way with modular systems, hardwired restrictions notwithstanding, it can be patched to any other module, too.

Let's say we patched it to the output volume. The sine wave which produced vibrato when applied to pitch would now produce a tremolo effect.

An LFO can also be patched into a filter to control the cutoff point. Using a sine wave set to 'vibrato' levels, this creates a subtle tonal change, not unlike a vibrato. At higher levels it creates more drastic tonal changes which are often referred to as growl. At lower frequencies, the LFO will move up and down the frequency range creating filter sweep effects.

In most systems, an LFO can also control the width of the pulse wave in the audio oscillator. As we saw in Chapter 3, changing the width of a pulse wave changes its harmonic content so this is another way to create dynamic tonal changes.

Music Note

Vibrato is a pitch variation while tremolo is a volume variation. The tremolo arm on a guitar is misnamed because it changes the pitch, not the volume

Glide, portamento and the slew limiter

One of the great features of analogue synthesisers is the ability to slide the pitch between notes, an effect without which no Dance record would be complete. It's a smooth slide, similar in effect to the very careful use of a pitch bend wheel. However, the slide in this case is totally automatic.

The effect is called glide or portamento, although hardware modules which perform this function are technical known as slew limiters. Many synths have a glide control, often in or near the oscillator section.

The main parameter is simply a control which sets the speed at which the pitch slides from one note to another. A comprehensive slew limiter might have separate controls for rising and falling pitches.

Velocity

Our final modulator in this chapter is velocity. It's not a module as such but a response of the amplifier to incoming note information. Nowadays we take velocity for granted and expect all keyboards to be velocity-sensitive and all sounds to respond to velocity information, but it's not so long ago that synthesisers were not velocity sensitive and there are still analogue models out there which don't respond to velocity.

If the synth responds to velocity you can use it in all sorts of ways, not just to control the volume of individual notes. If you route the velocity to the audio oscillator's pitch control, you could create a small increase in pitch when a key is struck sharply.

7

Experiments with a simple synthesiser

We're just about ready to put these modules together, plug them in and see what comes out the other end. But before we do, there are a couple of operating principles and another module we need to look at.

In preceding chapters we've blithely talked about patching one module to another – the LFO to the oscillator, for example – and we've explained that a key press triggers the start of an envelope's Attack phase. Now it's time to see how the patching is done.

Voltage control

In traditional analogue synthesisers it was done using voltages, a process which became known as voltage control. Although modern instruments may use digital circuits and numbers rather than voltages, the VC principle is still used, at least on the front end. This is also true of software synths.

One of the most popular methods of control is based on a 1 volt per octave (1v/oct) system where the difference between each note is 1/12th of a volt (there being 12 notes in an octave). When a key on a keyboard is pressed it generates a pitch control voltage which is fed to the audio oscillator which then generates a specific pitch. The keys higher and lower would generate 1/12th of a volt more or less.

Other voltage systems have been used but this remains the most popular. You don't really need to know which system your synth uses and in most hardwired synths you may not even be aware that voltage is being used to control the instrument.

It's worth pointing out that even though the 1v/oct system was popular, not all manufacturers who used it implemented it in the same way. There is no guarantee, therefore, that synth modules produced by different manufacturers, even if they are based on the same voltage control system, will work together. There are, however, companies such as Kenton Electronics (see the Appendix for details) that produce a range of kits which allow synthesisers from different manufacturers to work together.

In a modular synth, if the pitch CV actually patches into the oscillator there may be a control to determine how much of the signal gets through. What happens if we reduce this control so only half the voltage reaches the oscillator? Instead of an octave producing a one volt difference, it would require two octaves. Each key. therefore, would create a quarter tone change in pitch. How's that for an alternate tuning!

You may also be able to connect the CV to other modules, say to a low pass filter. The higher the note, the greater the voltage and the more the cutoff point will open, making the sound brighter.

Gates and triggers

Okay, that's how pitches are generated. But the keyboard also generates two other signals – a gate pulse and a trigger signal.

When a key is pressed the keyboard generates a gate pulse which lasts for the duration of the key press. Essentially, it's to let the synthesiser know that a key has been pressed and is being held down. It is most often used to trigger the envelope generator, and the envelope diagrams in Chapter 5 show that the gate pulse starts and ends when a key is pressed and released.

Some keyboards also generate a trigger signal which is a short on/off pulse each time a key is pressed. On hardwired synths and soft synths there may not be any need for this as it will be incorporated into the design. But with a modular synth, the trigger is used to tell the system that a new key has been pressed. It's usually fed into the ADSR to generate a new envelope. Without a trigger, if you held down a key and pressed another key, the new pitch would sound but without a new envelope.

You'll know if your synth has gate and trigger inputs. There may be separate outputs from the keyboard and some envelope generators may have a switch for selecting both gate and trigger signals or just the gate signal.

> ### INFO
>
> In most circumstances you will want to use both gate and trigger signals but switching off the trigger can produce interesting legato effects.

Voltage controlled everything

Now you know that voltages control everything, it will come as no surprise to learn that the main modules are called Voltage Controlled modules so we have the VCO (Voltage Controlled Oscillator), the VCF (Voltage Controlled Filter) and the VCA (Voltage Controlled Amplifier).

Even though modern synthesisers tend to use digital signals rather than voltages, many maintain the VC ethos and call their modules VCO, VCF and so on. In truth, it doesn't really matter how the modules control each other – they could use Smarties or quantum particles – the important thing is that control messages from any module can be used to control any other and that's what makes analogue and modular synthesis so interesting and exciting. But be aware that some synths call their modules 'Digitally Controlled' as in DCO and DCF, and some may not give them a prefix at all.

A basic synth patch

We'll now put everything together to make a basic synth patch which you can see in Figure 7.1. We'll be using similar diagrams

Figure 7.1 (right): A basic synth patch.

Figure 7.2 (below): Changing the ADSR settings can alter the character of the sound.

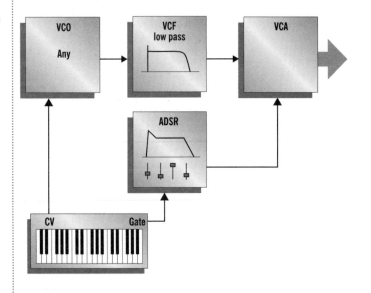

from here on in which should help you create the patches in any kind of synthesiser.

It's important to understand that no two synthesisers are alike and it's impossible to give a set of precise instructions which will produce exactly the same result across a range of instruments. The basic settings of all the modules will be included in the diagrams although you may have to twiddle a setting on your instrument here and there to get the desired result. But that's part of the fun.

This is a basic patch which is a good place to start when you want to create a new sound. Here's a quick check list of settings you might want to run through to make sure everything is working as it should.

- VCO. Make sure the CV input from the keyboard is reaching the oscillator and the keys are producing the correct pitches.
- VCF. Make sure the cutoff frequency control is open otherwise it could filter out the entire waveform.
- ADSR. Make sure the gate pulse is connected if this is necessary on your system. If all the ADSR controls are set to zero, the envelope generator will not produce any sound at all, so start with an 'average' envelope – fast Attack, medium Decay, half-way Sustain level, medium Release.
- VCA. The output is connected to speakers, isn't it...?

When you've produced a sound, experiment with the settings of the modules and see how they change it. Try different oscillators and filters to get a feel for the tones the synth can produce and then see how the envelope generator can change our perception of the sound. Try the ADSR settings in Figure 7.2. You'll find that with a pure tone such as a triangle wave, the various ADSR settings can make it wound like an organ, a flute or a piano.

Enveloping the filter

One of the characteristics of natural and instrumental sounds is that the tone often changes during the production of the sound. This is generally a decrease in the amplitude of the higher frequencies and it often follows the contour of the amplitude envelope. Isn't that convenient! It means we can achieve the same result by connecting the ADSR into the Filter as in Figure 7.3.

You need to patch the ADSR into the Filter's cutoff frequency control. Lower the cutoff a little and you'll hear that during the Attack phase, the filter opens making the sound brighter and then as the envelope and volume decrease, the filter will close reducing the higher frequencies.

Notice that the effect of the envelope is to raise the cutoff point as the envelope 'voltage' rises so if the cutoff point is initially set to full it will have nowhere to go and the sound won't change.

It's quite common to use a second envelope generator specifically for the filter, Figure 7.4, which means the tone does not have to follow the volume envelope.

INFO

Use longer Attack times for instrument sounds such as strings, and woodwind. This is a delicate setting; for a realistic sound you don't want to use a very long Attack time, just ease the control up from zero a little.

Figure 7.3: Connecting the ADSR to the Filter shapes tone in a similar way to the volume.

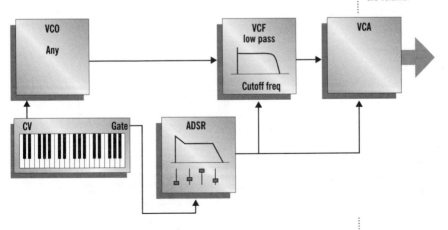

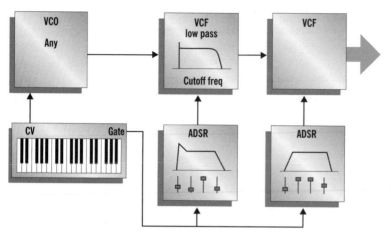

Figure 7.4: If the filter has
its own ADSR module, you
can shape the tone and
volume independently.

Fun with LFOs and the VCO

After experimenting with the basic synth patch, you'll have a good
feel for how the modules work and how they affect the sound. Now
let's add an LFO.

Figure 7.5 shows how to patch an LFO to the basic synth set up.
We're using a sine wave and we'll start by routing it to the VCO as
shown by the solid line. Set a rate (speed) to around 7Hz (7 cycles
per second) and experiment with the depth or range setting.

With a small depth setting the LFO will gently vary the pitch of
the VCO producing a musical vibrato. Increase the depth and it turns
into a siren! As you increase the rate, the vibrato will become
increasingly less musical and if the LFO can be turned up high
enough the output will be a sort of buzzing sound. Rate settings

Figure 7.5: Adding an LFO
to basic synth patch.

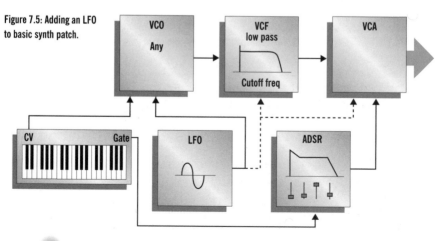

lower than 7Hz also detract from the musicality of the vibrato and become an undulation, not necessarily unpleasant but with less of a direct relationship to music as we're used to it.

Let's swap the sine wave for a sawtooth wave. Now the pitch rises, drops suddenly and starts rising again.

Let's try a square wave. Now instead of undulating, the pitch jumps between two frequencies. By carefully adjusting the depth setting you can make it oscillate between two pitches so pressing one key generates a trill effect.

The Keyboard Trigger

There's another control of interest here which the LFO may have and that's the Keyboard Trigger. This is simply an on/off switch which synchronises the start of the LFO to the press of a key on the keyboard. In other words, it ensures that the LFO waveform – and, in this case, the trill – starts at the beginning each time a key is pressed.

If your LFO does not have a Keyboard Trigger, it may well sync the two anyway. Without synchronisation, the LFO waveform will likely be at a different part of its cycle every time you press a key so the output and resulting sound would be different each time you play a note.

LFOs and filter sweeps

Disconnect the LFO from the VCO and connect it to the VCF to control the cutoff frequency, as shown by the dotted line. Set the cutoff control to about halfway. Try the same settings as before starting with a sine wave. This time the LFO cuts and boosts the frequencies to produce a filter sweep effect. If you had a steady hand you could produce a similar effect by raising and lowering the cutoff point manually.

The sawtooth produces another filter sweep effect with a drop at the end. Try a square wave. You can't create this effect manually because it makes the cutoff point jump between two settings.

Now, if your filter has an input for controlling resonance as well as the cutoff frequency, plug the LFO into that. As the voltage from the LFO increases (the rising section of a sine wave, for example), the resonance increases boosting the frequencies around the cutoff point. This produces another sweep effect and this technique is great for creating 'wha' sounds.

Shall we get a little more involved? Connect a second LFO to the filter's cutoff control. If the two LFOs have different settings, one will sweep the cutoff point up and down the frequency band while the other will sweep the resonance on-the-fly as it were. Nope, no idea what it'll sound like, depends on the settings, but it will produce some interesting sweep effects.

The LFO and the VCA

Okay, now disconnect that and patch the LFO into the amplifier, as shown by the second dotted line. The 'vibrato' sine wave setting will produce tremolo (see Chapter 6 for more about vibrato and tremolo). A sawtooth wave will ramp up the volume, drop it and so on, while a square wave will produce an oscillation between two volume levels.

Modulating the pulse width

Yet another use for the LFO is to use it to modulate the width of the pulse wave. In Figure 7.5, instead of connecting the LFO to the VCO's pitch input, connect it to the VCO's pulse wave modulation input (and select the pulse wave, of course) – although there's nothing to stop you connecting the LFO to the pitch input as well!

With a sine wave, this will smoothly change the pulse width – or the mark/space ratio to be technical – and, as we saw in Chapter 3, this in turn changes the harmonic content of the waveform which produces another sort of filter sweep effect. Although note that technically this is not cutting and boosting frequencies as a filter does but changing the frequencies which are generated. With gentle settings this can produce a sort of chorus effect which could be used for a string sound.

LFO delay

You can increase the authenticity of sounds such as strings by delaying the vibrato after pressing a key. String players often delay applying vibrato to inject a little more emotion in the sound. You can duplicate this if your LFO module has a delay control.

We need to link the delay to a key press and to do this we use exactly the same technique as we use with the envelope generator – the gate pulse. When a key is pressed, the LFO receives a gate pulse, the delay time starts ticking away and then the LFO's waveform begins. You can use delay with trills to good effect, too.

What if your LFO doesn't have a delay control? Is there another way to create a delay? Thanks to the flexibility of voltage control, there is. This may seem a little advanced but it still just uses the

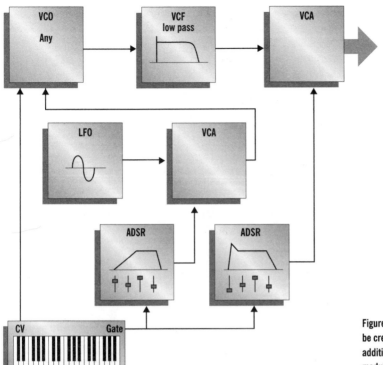

Figure 7.6: LFO delay can
be created using
additional VCA and ADSR
modules.

modules we've discussed so far and it demonstrates the flexibility of
the VC system. The patch is shown in Figure 7.6 and we need a
second ADSR and VCA. We connect the LFO output to the input of
the VCA and the output from the VCA into the VCO modulation
input, the input that the LFO would normally go to.

Now, when the VCA is open, the LFO signal will run straight
through and to the VCO. So, we use a second ADSR to control the
opening of the VCA. If the ADSR has a long Attack time, it will delay
the opening of the VCA and, hence, the onset of the LFO. The Attack
time determines the delay, the Sustain will determine the depth
(along with the LFO's own depth control). Make the Decay time the
same as the Decay in the ADSR which controls the sound's
amplitude.

Portamento, glide and the slew limiter

One of the great analogue effects of all time is the glide where the
pitch slides from one note to another. It's great fun to play and very
effective with bass lines and lead riffs.

Figure 7.7: Plugging a
glide module into a patch.

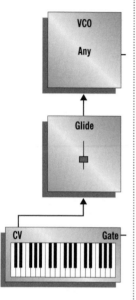

INFO

Some modules,
particularly slew limiters,
may have separate
settings for rise and fall
times. Some modules
have a gate input and
need a trigger like the
ADSR or LFO.

The easiest way to create it is with a glide, portamento or slew limiter module (we looked at these in Chapter 6). Essentially, it smoothes out differences between voltages arriving at its input. So if it receives two discrete voltages from a keyboard as would happen if you pressed two keys one after the other, it will output the first voltage and gradually increase the voltage output (or decrease it if the second voltage is lower than the first) until it reaches the second voltage. Patch this into an oscillator and the pitch will slide between the notes you play.

The patching arrangement is in Figure 7.7. It only shows the salient connections – the rest of the patch is exactly like those used earlier.

All glide modules have a rate or time control which determines how quickly the slide takes place. Short settings will scoop the pitch from one note to another; longer settings will, of course, take longer for the pitch to reach its destination.

Blocks of wood

So far, we've been experimenting with pitched sounds. We can make percussive, drum-type sounds using a noise waveform. The set up is essentially like the patches we've already used but with a noise waveform selected in the oscillator. Many synths have a separate noise generator which you connect just like an oscillator.

There's a patch to produce a wood block sound in Figure 7.8. You'll notice that we're using pink noise, but do try white noise – and any other shades of noise your synth may have – to hear the difference.

Although noise is unpitched, you can actually play the wood block sound via the filter. Connect the keyboard's CV to the filter so it controls the cutoff frequency as shown by the dotted line in Figure 7.8. Lower the cutoff frequency control in the filter and turn up the resonance a little.

Resonance emphasises the frequencies around the filter's cutoff point and the CV from the keyboard moves the cutoff point according to the notes being played so this will produced a pitched output.

The CV from the keyboard raises the cutoff point, so if you play high notes the voltage may try to move the cutoff point too much so the output won't be pitched. If this happens you simply need to lower the initial cutoff point a little more.

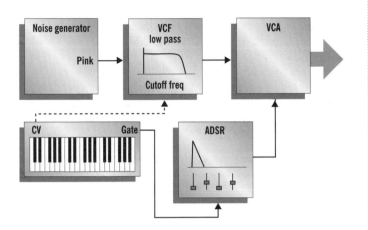

Key tracking

This leads us nicely into one more operation which we'll look at in this chapter. It's variously known as key tracking, key following, keyboard scaling or pitch scaling. Make up your own term!

With the patches we've used so far, the filter has stayed exactly the same whatever the pitch of the note. The tone of most acoustic instruments varies according to the pitch being played. For example, higher pitches tend to be brighter with more higher harmonics and applying the filter indiscriminately (as we have been doing) means that all notes across the spectrum have been filtered in exactly the same way.

For a touch more realism, we can increase the cutoff frequency as we increase the pitch. How? Simply by patching the CV from the keyboard into the filter. Experiment with the amount of CV going into the filter and with the initial cutoff setting. Some synths may have a built-in key tracking setting but it's easy enough to apply your own in this way.

You should now have a good understanding of the main synthesiser modules, what they do and some of the ways in which they can be patched together. One of the neat things about analogue synthesis and voltage control is that most outputs can be connected to most inputs. Experiment freely.

Although this chapter is called Experiments with a simple synthesiser, you will have discovered that using only very basic modules it's possible to create a vast range of sounds.

Additional modules

The modules we've looked at so far are the basic modules you'll find in every synth and although there are only a handful, we have already discovered that there are an enormous number of ways in which they can be linked together. In this chapter we'll explore some additional popular modules and suggest ways in which they can be used.

Although the modules we'll be looking at here could possibly be squeezed under the heading of 'advanced', you'll find them in most soft synths and many hardware synths, too.

Mixer

No prizes for guessing what this does! Mixers are used to combine signals from several sources. Many have level controls so you can balance the inputs but some may not and are simply used to merge several signals.

On most synths you can freely mix audio and control signals (providing the connections are there to allow you to do so) although this isn't always straightforward and the results aren't always predictable (see the Envelope follower module later in this chapter for more information about processing audio signals).

Some instruments may have an audio mixer for mixing audio signals and a separate control mixer for mixing control voltages. A major difference between the two is that the audio mixer probably has linear response level controls while the audio mixer has exponential or logarithmic controls. Here's a quick explanation of the difference.

Linear and logarithmic controls

A linear system simply adds the values of the incoming signals. If they were 1V, 2V and 4V the output would be 7V. However, we don't hear in a linear fashion but in a logarithmic fashion which means that the amplitude of an audio file has to be increased by several degrees of magnitude in order for us to perceive it at twice the volume. (Okay, that's a sort of watered-down version of the process but we don't want to get into any more scientific stuff here.) The point is, if your system has both audio and control mixers, use the right one for the job otherwise the results will not be as you expect.

Figure 8.1, shows a mixer being used to combine four waveforms in a simple form of additive synthesis. Use sine waves at different octaves, say 16', 8', 4' and 2'. Adjust the input levels in the mixer and see how the output changes. Set the 16' sine wave to full, the 8' to 1/2 volume, the 4' to 1/3 and the 2' to 1/4. It should sound

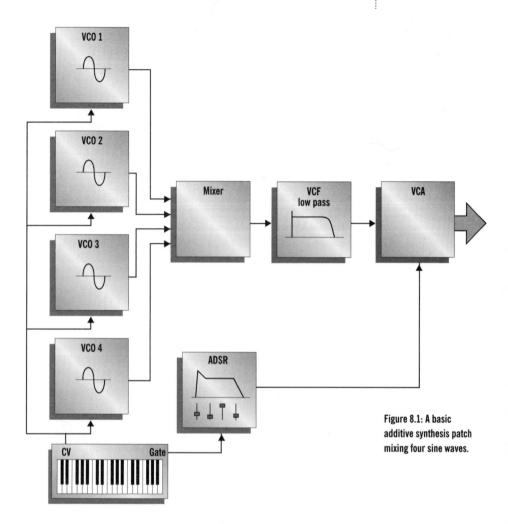

Figure 8.1: A basic additive synthesis patch mixing four sine waves.

vaguely like a sawtooth (refer to Chapter 3 for more information about the harmonic content of waveforms). Try different combinations of levels. Try different waveforms.

You can create a chimes patch by tuning the oscillators to different initial pitches. Set VCO 1 to 8' and VCO 2 to 4'. Set VCO 3 to 16' but increase the pitch by four semitones so instead of playing C when a C key is pressed on the keyboard, it plays the E above it. Set VCO 4 to 4' but increase the pitch by five semitones so instead of playing a C it plays the F above. You might have to balance the volumes but that should give you an interesting chimes/tubular bells-type sound.

Another use for a mixer is to provide more inputs to a module which has only one or two. Let's say the filter cutoff frequency has only one input but you want to control it from an ADSR, an LFO and the keyboard. No problem – run the three outputs into a mixer and connect the mixer output to the filter.

Inverter

The inverter is an interesting chap, not often found on hardwired synths but quite popular on hardware modular synths and modular soft synths. Quite simply, it inverts the incoming signal so if the input was 5V, the output would be –5V and so on.

Some hardware synthesisers, particularly modular ones, have an inverted output in the envelope module. Otherwise, any signal can be inverted by passing it through an inverter. There are rarely any controls although occasionally you may come across a mixer with an inverted output in which case there may be controls on the mixer

Figure 8.2: The inverted output of an ADSR module.

to balance the relative signal inputs. Figure 8.2 shows what the inverted output of an ADSR module is like.

Inverted signals can be used for all sorts of tricks. If we use a normal envelope like the one in Figure 8.2, to control a filter's cutoff point, the sound starts bright and then grows duller as it progresses, becoming increasingly dull during the Release phase. If we applied the inverted envelope to the filter, the sound would start off dull and then become brighter as it gets softer.

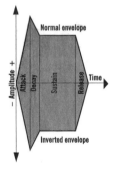

You can route an inverted envelope to most places you can route a normal envelope. Use it to control the filter's resonance, to control the width of a pulse wave, to scoop the pitch up – or down – in a VCO, or to control the VCA. Figure 8.3 shows how an inverted ADSR can be used to lower a pitch and slide it up again to create the sort of scoop-up pitch effect you get when you whistle (well, the way some people whistle).

The main variation on the basic patches in the previous chapter is an inverted envelope. The envelope has a zero Attack time so it jumps straight up to the Attack level then the Decay reduces it, not too slowly. If this were to be applied to the VCO, it would raise the pitch. Inverted, however, it immediately lowers the pitch and then slides it up to its normal level. The VCO input control determines the starting pitch and the Decay time determines the length of the slide.

One more idea – inverting an LFO to create a stereo pan effect, Figure 8.4. This is just a simple example and we only show the 'working bits' but you can see that the output from the LFO is fed to one VCA and the inverted output is fed to another VCA. When the normal LFO is fully positive, the VCA it controls will be fully open,

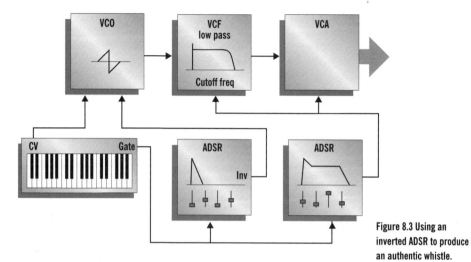

Figure 8.3 Using an
inverted ADSR to produce
an authentic whistle.

while the inverted signal will cause the other VCA to be fully closed. As the normal LFO output moves through its cycle it will slowly close the VCA while the inverted signal will slowly open the other VCA creating a panning effect.

We've suggested an LFO rate of 1Hz to produce a sweep but you can alter this to suit. Higher rates will create a stereo tremolo effect. If the panning is too extreme, you can reduce it by increasing the VCA input controls so there is always some level of output at both left and right VCAs.

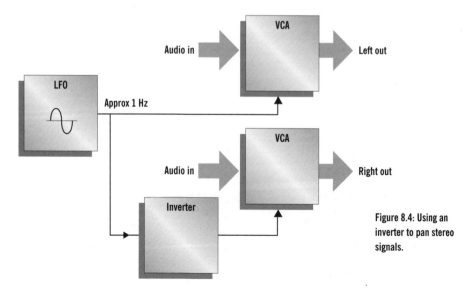

Figure 8.4: Using an
inverter to pan stereo
signals.

Envelope follower

In the mixer section earlier we said that many synthesisers allow you to combine audio and control signals but because of their differences the results may not always be predictable. There is a module designed to bridge the gap and that's the envelope follower.

This essentially removes the 'sound' from a waveform and outputs its volume contour or envelope which can be fed into the synthesiser. Figure 8.5 shows what it does. The envelope can be used to control synth modules to produce all sorts of effects.

At its simplest, the volume of the audio signal can control the volume of the synth – or virtually any other aspect of the synth for that matter. It can make the output level of the synth 'follow' the incoming audio level. Taking this a stage further it can be used to create a 'ducking' effect where an incoming audio signal automatically reduces the volume of the synth. This is commonly used by DJs; when they speak, the volume of the music is automatically lowered. You can feed a synthesised waveform into it, too, and it would 'smooth' it.

Obviously, the envelope follower has an audio input and it's designed to interface with the real world, it might have both mic and line inputs. The mic input would be used with sounds from low level instruments such as a microphone or electric guitar – unamplified, of course!

Some also have a gate and trigger output. These normally work on a threshold basis and there'll be a threshold control so you can decide at what level the incoming signal generates these pulses. The gate and trigger pulses can be used in exactly the same way as the pulses generated by a keyboard (refer to the previous chapter for more information about gates and triggers). You should also be able to route the audio input through the module to, say a VCA.

Figure 8.6 shows a basic patch whereby the volume of the incoming audio signal is used to filter it. Let's follow the logic through the patch. First of all, the audio signal is passed through the envelope follower to the VCF and then the VCA, just like the output from an oscillator. The follower's envelope output (which

Figure 8.5: An envelope follower picks out the volume changes from an audio signal

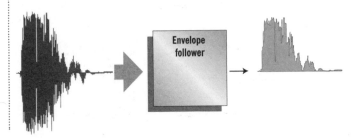

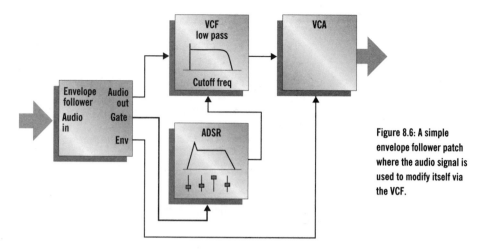

Figure 8.6: A simple envelope follower patch where the audio signal is used to modify itself via the VCF.

follows the volume contour of the audio signal) is routed to the VCA and acts as an ADSR module. This should cause the audio signal to pass through the system at roughly the same volume as it entered it.

Finally, the gate output from the follower is routed to an ADSR module which is used to vary the cutoff frequency of the filter. The level or sensitivity of the signal which produces the gate output is determined by the threshold control so at one extreme it would trigger virtually all the time and at the other it would only trigger, if at all, when the incoming audio was very loud.

Figure 8.7 shows how an envelope follower could be used to make an audio signal reduce the amplitude of another audio signal. This is known as ducking because the sound 'ducks' as if to avoid the incoming signal.

The output from the main audio source (which could be music or

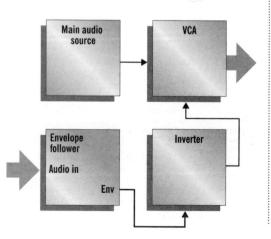

Figure 8.7: Using an envelope follower and an inverter to create a ducking effect.

even the output from a synth patch) is fed into a VCA. The envelope follower's envelope output is again used to control this VCA as in Figure 8.6. However, it first runs through an inverter which means that when the audio signal is quiet, the envelope outputs a normal signal which lets the main audio source pass through the VCA.

When the audio signal increases in volume, the inverted envelope reduces the level of the signal going into the VCA and so the output level of the main audio source is reduced.

Sub oscillators and dividers

A sub oscillator is simply an oscillator which adds an additional pitch to the output, usually one or two octaves below the pitch of the main oscillator. Some hardware synths have a sub oscillator switch (which many users leave in the On position permanently). It adds more depth – read bass – to a sound and is great for speaker-shaking Dance music.

Sub oscillators were an easy – and cheap – way to add more sonic variety to a synth and you'll still find them on hardware synths for this reason. But with soft synths and their unlimited supply of modules there is no need to save costs and it's easy to add another oscillator or two – or more – to a patch and lower the octave settings on them to provide some oomph. Great for phat bass lines.

Most sub oscillators add a fixed waveform such as a sawtooth or square wave to the output. However, some actually generate sub-octave frequencies from the original frequency and these are technically known as frequency dividers. They may output one, two or even four sub frequencies, each one an octave lower than the other. You may also find a module which can create sub-harmonics (as opposed to straight octaves) from a signal although these are less common.

Each output should have a level control, and all the sub frequencies along with the original input are usually summed in one output, again with a volume control. As well as using this to beef up an oscillator output, you can use it to create new tones by mixing the four outputs in various combinations. Try it with various waveforms.

Do try this at home

Here's a bit of a wacky patch, Figure 8.8. It uses a divider to divide an audio signal which should be monophonic and fairly clean such as a flute, a vocal pitch, a single guitar note and so on. The audio is routed through an envelope follower and then to a VCF where a little filtering may improve the quality of the division. If everything works

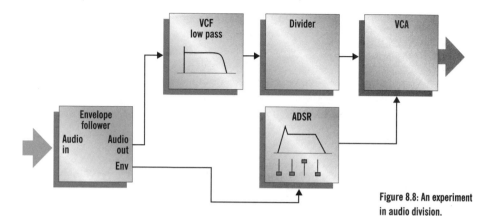

Figure 8.8: An experiment in audio division.

fine, you could patch another controller into the filter such as an LFO.

The follower's envelope output feeds the ADSR which controls the VCA. The follower's threshold needs to be fairly high. It's a bit of an experimental patch – so experiment.

Ring modulation

The ring modulator has long been used to create all sorts of synthy, other-world effects. It can be used with oscillators to create metallic sounds such as bells and chimes but it's also great at doing weird things to audio – everything from vocals to acoustic instruments.

A ring modulator has two inputs and one output. It rarely has any additional controls. The output is a combination of the sum and the difference of the two input frequencies. So, if we grab a calculator (or are just plain good at sums) we can work this out as follows...

We'll try to keep it musical. Refer to the table overleaf. Let's say we input two frequencies – the A above Middle C which has a frequency of 440Hz and the C above it which has a frequency of 523.25Hz. The sum is 963.25Hz and the difference is 83.25Hz, so these two frequencies appear at the output. However, these are not the exact frequencies of any of the notes in our Western scale. 963.25Hz falls between Bb5 at 932.33Hz and B5 at 987.77Hz. The nearest to 83.25Hz is E2 at 82.407Hz.

The sound they produce, therefore, is slightly dissonant and contains harmonics which are not part of the natural harmonic series, often with a metallic edge to it.

It's worth touching on a couple of things here about frequencies and the notes in our Western scale – basically, there is no 'even number' correlation. Apart from the As in our scale, the frequencies

INFO

See Chapter 3 for more about harmonics

Note (MIDI no.)	Freq (Hz)	Note (MIDI no.)	Freq (Hz)	Note (MIDI no.)	Freq (Hz)
C-2 (0)	8.176	G1 (43)	97.999	D5 (86)	1174.7
C#-2 (1)	8.662	G#1 (44)	103.83	D#5 (87)	1244.5
D-2 (2)	9.177	A1 (45)	110.00	E5 (88)	1318.5
D#-2 (3)	9.723	A#1 (46)	116.54	F5 (89)	1396.9
E-2 (4)	10.301	B1 (47)	123.47	F#5 (90)	1480.0
F-2 (5)	10.914	C2 (48)	130.81	G5 (91)	1568.0
F#-2 (6)	11.563	C#2 (49)	138.59	G#5 (92)	1661.2
G-2 (7)	12.205	D2 (50)	146.83	A5 (93)	1760.0
G#-2 (8)	12.979	D#2 (51)	155.56	A#5 (94)	1864.7
A-2 (9)	13.750	E2 (52)	164.81	B5 (94)	1975.5
A#-2 (10)	14.568	F2 (53)	174.61	C6 (96)	2093.0
B-2 (11)	15.434	F#2 (54)	185.00	C#6 (97)	2217.5
C-2 (12)	16.352	G2 (55)	196.00	D6 (98)	2349.3
C#-1 (13)	17.324	G#2 (56)	207.65	D#6 (99)	2489.0
D-1 (14)	18.354	A2 (57)	220.00	E6 (100)	2637.0
D#-1 (15)	19.446	A#2 (58)	233.08	F6 (101)	2793.8
E-1 (16)	20.602	B2 (59)	246.94	F#6 (102)	2960.0
F-1 (17)	21.827	**C3 (60) Mid C**	**261.63**	G6 (103)	3136.0
F#-1 (18)	23.125	C#3 (61)	277.18	G#6 (104)	3322.4
G-1 (19)	24.410	D3 (62)	293.66	A6 (105)	3520.0
G#-1 (20)	25.957	D#3 (63)	311.13	A#6 (106)	3729.3
A-1 (21)	27.500	E3 (64)	329.63	B6 (107)	3951.1
A#-1 (22)	29.135	F3 (65)	349.23	C7 (108)	4186.0
B-1 (23)	30.868	F#3 (66)	369.99	C#7 (109)	4435.0
C0 (24)	32.703	G3 (67)	392.00	D7 (110)	4698.6
C#0 (25)	34.648	G#3 (68)	414.30	D#7 (111)	4978.0
D0 (26)	36.708	A3 (69)	440.00	E7 (112)	5274.0
D#0 (27)	38.891	A#3 (70)	466.16	F7 (113)	5587.6
E0 (28)	41.203	B3 (71)	493.88	F#7 (114)	5920.0
F0 (29)	43.654	C4 (72)	523.25	G7 (115)	6272.0
F#0 (30)	46.249	C#4 (73)	554.37	G#7 (116)	6644.8
G0 (31)	48.999	D4 (74)	587.33	A7 (117)	7040.0
G#0 (32)	51.913	D#4 (75)	622.25	A#7 (118)	7458.6
A0 (33)	55.000	E1 (76)	659.26	B7 (119)	7902.2
A#0 (34)	58.270	F4 (77)	698.46	C8 (120)	8372.0
B0 (35)	61.735	F#4 (78)	739.99	C#8 (121)	8870.0
C1 (36)	65.406	G4 (79)	783.99	D8 (122)	9397.2
C#1 (37)	69.296	G#4 (80)	830.61	D#8 (123)	9956.0
D1 (38)	73.416	A4 (81)	880.00	E8 (124)	10548.0
D#1 (39)	77.782	A#4 (82)	932.33	F8 (125)	11175.2
E1 (40)	82.407	B4 (83)	987.77	F#8 (126)	11840.0
F1 (41)	87.307	C5 (84)	1046.5	G8 (127)	12543.9
F#1 (42)	92.499	C#5 (85)	1108.7		

of most of the other notes are not even-numbered Hertz so adding and subtracting note-based frequencies will not produce frequencies which are perfectly in tune. In the vast majority of cases, the frequencies generated by a ring modulator will be 'in the cracks'.

Figure 8.9 illustrates a basic ring modulation patch which combines two sine waves to produce a metallic sound like a bell or a chime or a glock. It should have a short Attack time and long Release and Decay times.

Now comes the tricky bit – tuning the oscillators. You don't have to tune them but, as we've discovered, the relationship between the input frequencies is crucial so a little experimentation is in order. Often, the best results – that is, the most musical – will come when the input frequencies have a close harmonic relationship to each other. The notes in the Western scale as she is tuned, do not.

TIP

Here's another ring modulation experimental suggestion – try applying an LFO (at all rates from very slow to fast) to one or both the oscillators before they hit the ring modulator.

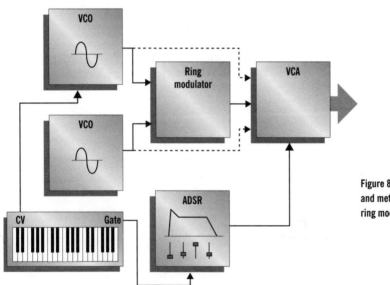

Figure 8.9: Creating bells and metallic sounds with ring modulation.

A brief excursion into just intonation

This is more by way of an aside as we're moving beyond the scope of this book but it's interesting and relevant to the use of ring modulators.

You may have heard of just intonation. This is the process of tuning each note in a scale so it fits the natural harmonic series. It produces a scale where the notes have a more natural and 'perfect' harmonic relationship to each other and it was used in music up until the 18th century. The trouble is, the frequencies of the notes in one scale are not necessarily the same as the frequencies of the notes in another scale.

For example, if we compare the D in the key of F major to the D in the key of B minor, the second A is slightly flatter. If we try to notate the frequencies in a scale of just intonation, we find that we have more than 12 intervals and there is a difference between a semitone and a minor tone!

You'll be pleased to hear that this is as far as we're going with just intonation but for reference we'll list the most common intervals in a 'Western' scale along with their ratios.

Note in 'scale' of C	Interval	Ratio
C	Unison	1:1
D	Major second	9:8
Eb	Minor third	6:5
E	Major third	5:4
F	Perfect fourth	4:3
G	Perfect fifth	3:2
Ab	Minor sixth	8:5
A	Major sixth	5:3
B	Major seventh	15:8
C	Octave	2:1

Note, that because all the pitches in a just intonation scale have a specific ratio to each other, the frequency of any pitch can easily be calculated. To build a scale starting with our friend A at 440Hz we simply use the ratios. The major third above it would be 550 (440/4*5), the seventh would be 825 (440/8*15) and so on.

A good instrumentalist playing through different keys would automatically adjust his or her playing to compensate. However, this is not possible with fixed-pitch instruments such as the harpsichord and organ so the scale of equal temperament was devised whereby an octave was divided precisely into 12 steps so the difference between each semitone was exactly the same.

INFO

J.S. Bach wrote a set of 48 Preludes and Fugues to celebrate equal temperament called the Well Tempered Clavier.

On the beat

So, the point of all this is that tuning the oscillators to the natural harmonic series may produce more 'harmonic' results. That's all!

You can manually – and aurally – tune oscillators by listening carefully to the two pitches (it helps if you use sine waves). If they are 'out of natural harmony' you will hear a slight pulsing, a wavering of loudness, known as a beat. The more consonant the interval (such as an octave, a fifth or a sixth), the easier it is to detect the beats.

The beats are the difference in frequency between the natural harmonic relationship of the two pitches. So, if we were tuning A at 440Hz with 660Hz which is a perfect fifth higher, and the oscillator was actually playing 658Hz, we'd hear a beat with a frequency of 2Hz.

If you can specify the frequencies of the oscillators in your synth by entering the numbers in Hertz directly, it'll save you tuning up.

So, in the patch in Figure 8.9 try tuning the oscillators to a natural harmonic interval such as a perfect fifth, a minor third or an octave. Then tune them to the frequencies used by the notes in the Western scale and listen to the difference.

Do note, of course, that if you use the patch to play a tune, each note will produce a different set of output frequencies... But experiment, that's the name of the game. You can stabilise the pitch a little by adding the direct output from either or both the oscillators as shown by the dotted lines in Figure 8.9.

You can route waveforms other than sine waves to a ring modulator. Each harmonic in one wave will react with each of the harmonics in the other to produce some interesting sounds.

Sample and hold

The sample and hold module was a favourite among early synthesists for producing a range of pitched and timbral effects, and it's still a great module to play with. As its name suggests it samples an incoming signal and holds it until it's told to sample another one.

All S&H units have an input for the signal to be sampled and an output for the sampled signal. It will also have an input for a trigger signal or clock pulse which tells it when to take a sample, and some units may have an internal clock such as an LFO which does this. It may also have a clock output which it transmits each time the output changes and this would typically be used to trigger an envelope generator.

Let's see it in action. Say you feed it a sawtooth waveform and apply a regular clock pulse, Figure 8.10. When the pulse triggers the unit, it samples the current value of the waveform and holds it until the next pulse comes along at which time it resamples the waveform, holds it and so on.

The output is a voltage, of course, and can be applied to any synth module. Feed it to an oscillator and it will generate a series of pitches. Feed it to a filter and it will make the cutoff point jump around creating a series of interesting tonal changes.

TIP

One of the most interesting things you can do with ring modulation is to use an audio input as one of the sources. Vocals are great fun but you can use any audio signal at all. Use an envelope follower as described earlier to produce an envelope from the sound.

INFO

We've used a sawtooth in these examples but different waveforms will produce different patterns. If the sawtooth produces rising arpeggios, a sine or triangle wave would produce up and down arpeggios. A square wave, however, will produce only two pitches. A pulse wave will also produce two pitches but the pulse width will determine how many high and how many low are in the pattern.

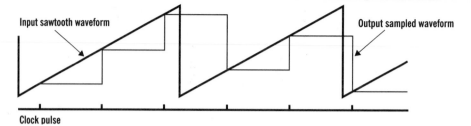

Input sawtooth waveform

Output sampled waveform

Clock pulse

Figure 8.10: How a sample and hold module works.

Figure 8.11: Doubling the sample rate can change the pattern of the notes generated.

You can see from our little example that simply changing the frequency of the pulses will change the pattern of the output. If the output was applied to pitches the result might be something like the first example in Figure 8.11. If the pulse rate was doubled, the pattern might be similar to that in the second example.

If the clock rate is not an exact multiple of the frequency of the sampled waveform then the output will not produce a regular pattern – as in these examples. By adjusting both the frequency of the sample source and the clock rate, it's possible to produce a vast number of non-repeating patterns or patterns which repeat every so-often.

Of course, we don't have to sample a regular waveform. We could sample a noise waveform which would result in a random output – a great favourite among synthesists. It need not result in cacophony. If the clock rate is fast and the oscillator set to a high pitch range, the output will be high-pitched tinkling sounds.

Figure 8.12 shows a basic sample and hold patch suitable for experimenting with pitched output. You could plug a filter into the circuit between the VCO and VCA if you wish. LFO 1 provides the sample source although you could plug anything in here from a regular oscillator to a noise generator or even the output from an ADSR unit.

LFO 2 generates the clock pulse telling the S&H unit when to take a sample. This will usually be set to a square wave (or a pulse wave) so the high of the wave provides enough voltage to trigger the unit.

Of course, the clock pulses don't have to be regular. There are several ways to introduce a random pulse to the patch. One would be to feed noise into the S&H's trigger input and adjust the levels so it would only trigger at high (but random) voltages. Another way would be to use noise to control the width of a pulse wave in an LFO. It's amazing what you can do with voltages.

Some synthesiser systems may have a quantizer module which converts an incoming voltage to the nearest voltage required to produce a correctly-tuned note. If you want to produce pitched output this can be a very powerful addition to your set up and it may offer the choice of different scales such as major, minor, chromatic and pentatonic.

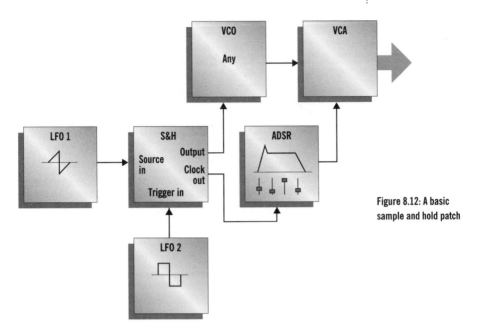

Figure 8.12: A basic sample and hold patch

For a variation on the pitched theme, patch a slew limiter between the S&H's output and the oscillator and listen to the pitches swoop up and down.

Another interesting S&H effect is to use it to control a filter, Figure 8.13. There are several variations you can implement on this idea. The example continuously varies the filter and when you press a key you will hear the tone being, er, continuously varied throughout the duration of the note.

If you patch the keyboard's gate output to the S&H's trigger, then the S&H will only be triggered once which is when the key is pressed. The tone won't vary during the duration of the note but each note will have a different tone colour.

Another idea is to patch a slew limiter between the S&H and the VCF input to produce filter sweep effects.

Taking the filter control idea a step further – although this may not be everyone's cup of cocoa – if you could connect the S&H output to the VCO instead of the filter, every key press will produce a different note.

INFO

The output voltages from a sample and hold module are most unlikely to produce notes in the Western scale. However, it's surprising how often an 'out of tune' arpeggio can add to the appeal of a piece of music.

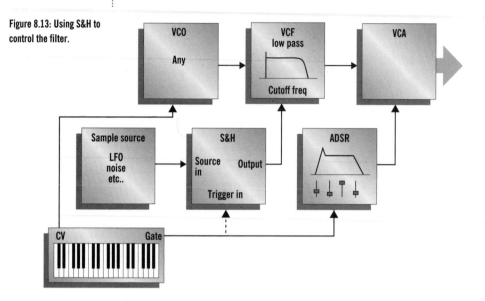

Figure 8.13: Using S&H to control the filter.

That's the end of this *Quick Guide*. We've looked at all the basic modules you'll find in most synthesisers and you will have discovered that even these few modules can produce a vast range of sounds and effects. You now have an excellent understanding of how analogue synthesis works and will be able to construct patches of your own on virtually any analogue synth which is modelled on the Control Voltage principle.

Keep patching and have fun!

T here are so many synth resources on the Web that it would take another book to list them all! So this list is intended to be representative, not comprehensive.

The Synth resources on the Web section includes sites which have links to all the major resources – and many 'hidden' ones.

Synth resources on the Web

120 Years of Electronic Music (www.obsolete.com/120_years/) A history of electronic musical instruments.
Harmony Central (www.harmony-central.com/Synth/Data) A large database of synths and reviews.
Keyboard Museum (www.keyboardmuseum.org) Pictures, information and sounds of all sorts of synths.
Music Machine (http://machines.hyperreal.org) A host of musical electronica.
Synth Zone (www.synthzone.com) Umpteen pages of links and information on all things synthy.
Synthesizer Picture Archive (www.code404.com/synths) Not just pictures but lots of useful analogue synth links.
Synthmuseum (www.synthmuseum.com) A huge database of info about vintage electronic musical instruments.
Vintage Synth Explorer (www.vintagesynth.com) A resource of info on over 400 vintage and retro synths.

Analogue synth manufacturers

Analogue Solutions (www.analoguesolutions.com) Concussor modular synthesiser systems.
Clavia (www.clavia.se) Manufacturer of the Nord Modular range of synths.
Creamware (www.creamware.com) Pulsar range of analogue software-based synths on PCI cards for Mac and PC.
Doepfer (www.doepfer.de) Manufacturer of dedicated analogue synth modules and systems. This is the real thing.
Future Retro (www.angelfire.com/biz2/FutureRetro/) Manufacturer of the 777 monophonic analogue synth.
Korg (www.korg.co.uk) Manufacturer of stylish musical instruments.
Roland UK (www.roland.co.uk) Major synth manufacturer.
Technosaurus (www.technosaurus.ch) More real analogue modular synth systems.
Waldorf (www.waldorf-gmbh.de) Manufacturer of hardware analogue synths and developer of soft synth versions.
Yamaha (www.yamaha.co.uk) Largest musical instrument manufacturer in the world.

Analogue synth-friendly companies

Analogue Modular Systems (www.analogsynths.com) USA-based company specialising in analogue synths.
Kenton Electronics (www.kenton.co.uk) Manufactures boxes and retrofit units for controlling analogue synths .

Soft synths

Access Music (www.access-music.de) Hardware analogue synths and software versions, too.
Applied Acoustics (www.applied-acoustics.com) Tassman, physical modelling of analogue hardware.
BitHeadz (www.bitheadz.com) Soft synths – Retro analogue synth, Unity sample player, Voodoo drum machine.
Dr Sync (www.mtu-net.ru/syncmodular) SynC Modular, a modular soft synth.
Emagic (www.emagic.de) Logic Audio developer, plus ES-1 soft synth and EXS24 soft sampler.
Koblo (www.koblo.com) Vibra, Stella and Gamma – synths, samplers and drum machines in software.
Native Instruments (www.nativeinstruments.com) Reaktor and Dynamo soft synths, B4 tone wheel organ synth.
Properllerhead (www.propellerheads.se) Developers of ReBirth and Reason, a rack-based modular synth.
Rave Technologies (www.audioarchitect.com) Audio Architect modular synth.
Seer Systems (www.seersystems.com) Reality and SurReal soft synths.
Software Technology (www.software-technology.com) The Vaz range of soft modular synths.
SoundsLogical (www.soundslogical.com) WaveWarp soft synth and audio processor.
Steinberg (www.steinberg.de) Cubase developer, plus several VST Instrument soft synths.
UltraMaster (www.ultramaster.com) Software emulation of the Roland Juno 6.

Index